Learning to Read, Step by Step!

Ready to Read **Preschool–Kindergarten**
• big type and easy words • rhyme and rhythm • picture clues
For children who know the alphabet and are eager to begin reading.

Reading with Help **Preschool–Grade 1**
• basic vocabulary • short sentences • simple stories
For children who recognize familiar words and sound out new words with help.

Reading on Your Own **Grades 1–3**
• engaging characters • easy-to-follow plots • popular topics
For children who are ready to read on their own.

Reading Paragraphs **Grades 2–3**
• challenging vocabulary • short paragraphs • exciting stories
For newly independent readers who read simple sentences with confidence.

Ready for Chapters **Grades 2–4**
• chapters • longer paragraphs • full-color art
For children who want to take the plunge into chapter books but still like colorful pictures.

STEP INTO READING® is designed to give every child a successful reading experience. The grade levels are only guides; children will progress through the steps at their own speed, developing confidence in their reading. The F&P Text Level on the back cover serves as another tool to help you choose the right book for your child.

Remember, a lifetime love of reading starts with a single step!

To those who remember and to the memory of Gogisgi/Carroll Arnett, Cherokee poet and teacher, who first showed that trail to me

Ktsi wliwini, great thanks, to my many Aniyunwiya friends and teachers over the years. Thank you for your patience with me. I am especially grateful to those Cherokee writers and storytellers who read this manuscript in its early stages and offered such good advice. In particular, I want to acknowledge my dear friends Geary Hobson, Gayle Ross, Murv Jacob, Marilou Awiakta, and Robert Conley. Wado, wado. The Principal People will survive.

—J.B.

 Published in the United States by Random House Children's Books, a division of Random House LLC, a Penguin Random House Company, New York.

Visit us on the Web!
StepIntoReading.com
randomhousekids.com

Educators and librarians, for a variety of teaching tools, visit us at
RHTeachersLibrarians.com

Library of Congress Cataloging-in-Publication Data
Bruchac, Joseph, 1942– .
The Trail of Tears / by Joseph Bruchac ; illustrated by Diana Magnuson.
p. cm. — (Step into reading. A step 5 book)
Summary: Recounts how the Cherokees, after fighting to keep their land in the nineteenth century, were forced to leave and travel 1,200 miles to a new settlement in Oklahoma, a terrible journey known as the Trail of Tears.
ISBN 978-0-679-89052-2 (trade) — ISBN 978-0-679-99052-9 (lib. bdg.) —
ISBN 978-0-385-37473-6 (ebook)
1. Trail of Tears, 1838– —Juvenile literature.
2. Cherokee Indians—History—19th century—Juvenile literature.
3. Cherokee Indians—Relocation—Juvenile literature.
I. Magnuson, Diana, ill. II. Title. III. Series: Step into reading. Step 5 book.
E99.C5 B888 2003 975.0049755—dc21 2002014929

Printed in the United States of America 34 33 32 31 30 29 28 27 26

This book has been officially leveled by using the F&P Text Level Gradient™ Leveling System.

STEP INTO READING®

A HISTORY READER

The Trail of Tears

By Joseph Bruchac
Illustrated by Diana Magnuson

Random House New York

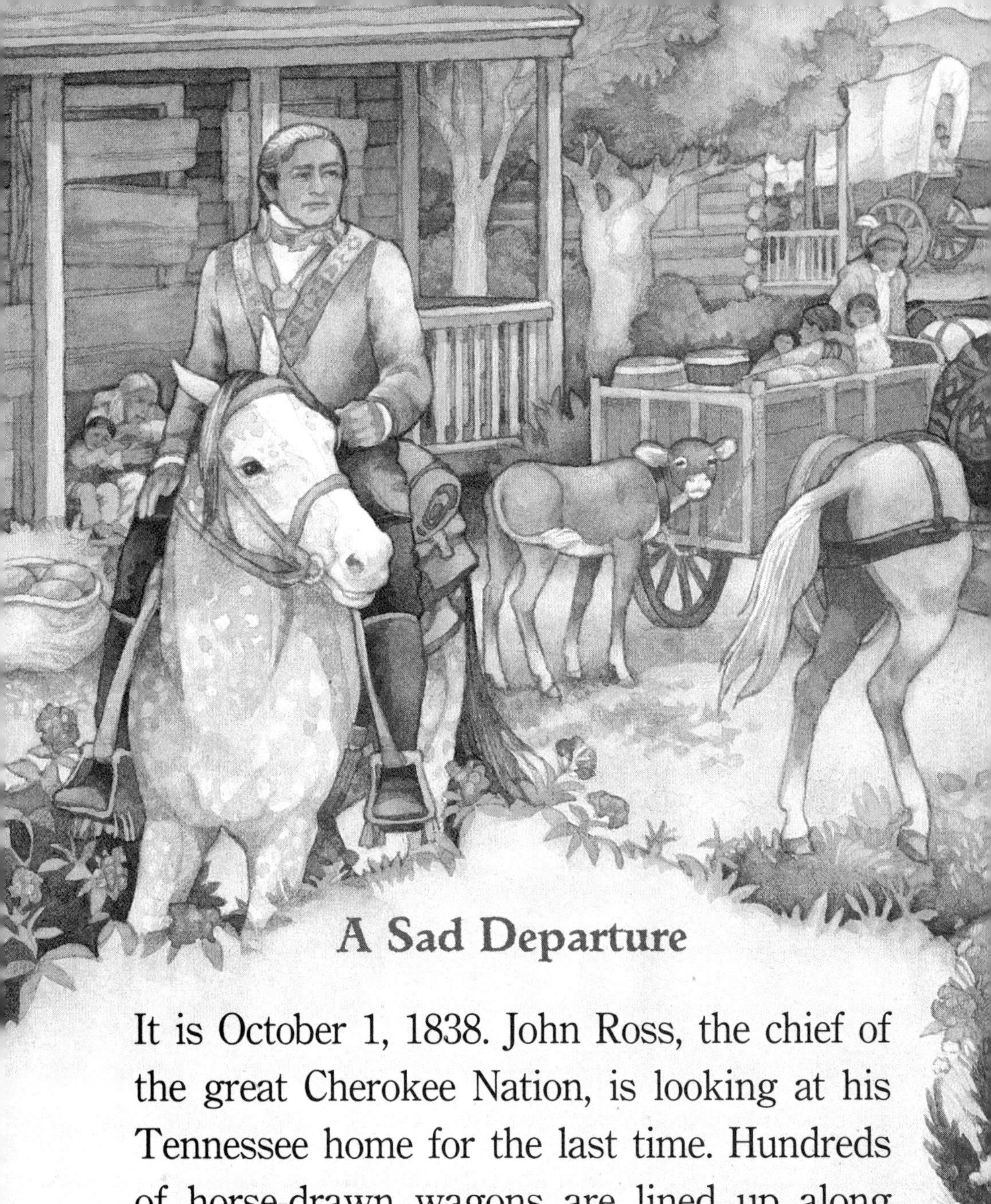

A Sad Departure

It is October 1, 1838. John Ross, the chief of the great Cherokee Nation, is looking at his Tennessee home for the last time. Hundreds of horse-drawn wagons are lined up along the Hiwassee River. All around him, other Cherokees have finished packing their belongings. It is time to go.

John Ross is worried. His people do not have enough food or blankets. Many of them are ill. All of them are filled with sorrow. John Ross thinks of all they are leaving behind. He remembers the schools and houses and farms the Cherokees built. He and his people do not want to leave their homes. But they have no choice. The 17,000 people of the Cherokee Nation must go west.

John Ross climbs on a wagon. The people gather around him as he says a short prayer in Cherokee. "We ask for God's guidance on our journey," he says. "Amen," say the people in reply.

A bugle is sounded. The drivers urge their teams forward. Suddenly, a roll of thunder is heard. A black cloud appears in the western sky. Many Cherokees shake their heads. They fear it is an omen of bad luck. Their long journey will be a hard one.

A Civilized Tribe

Who are the Cherokees and why must they go west?

The Cherokees were living in America long before the first white colonists arrived. Their oldest stories tell how earth was shaped by the flight of the Great Buzzard. He flew low over the new land to dry it with his wings, pushing down the valleys and lifting up the hills and peaks of the Great Smoky Mountains. Then two people emerged from the earth. They were Kanati and Selu, the first man and woman. All Cherokees are their children.

This story shows how connected the Cherokees feel to their land. It is a part of them.

What we know as Georgia, Alabama, Tennessee, Kentucky, South Carolina, and North Carolina were all once Cherokee land. Each Cherokee town had its own leaders, chosen by the people. They proudly called themselves *Ani'-Yun'wiya*—"the Principal People." (The name Cherokee comes from *jilagi*—a Creek Indian word meaning "People of Different Speech.")

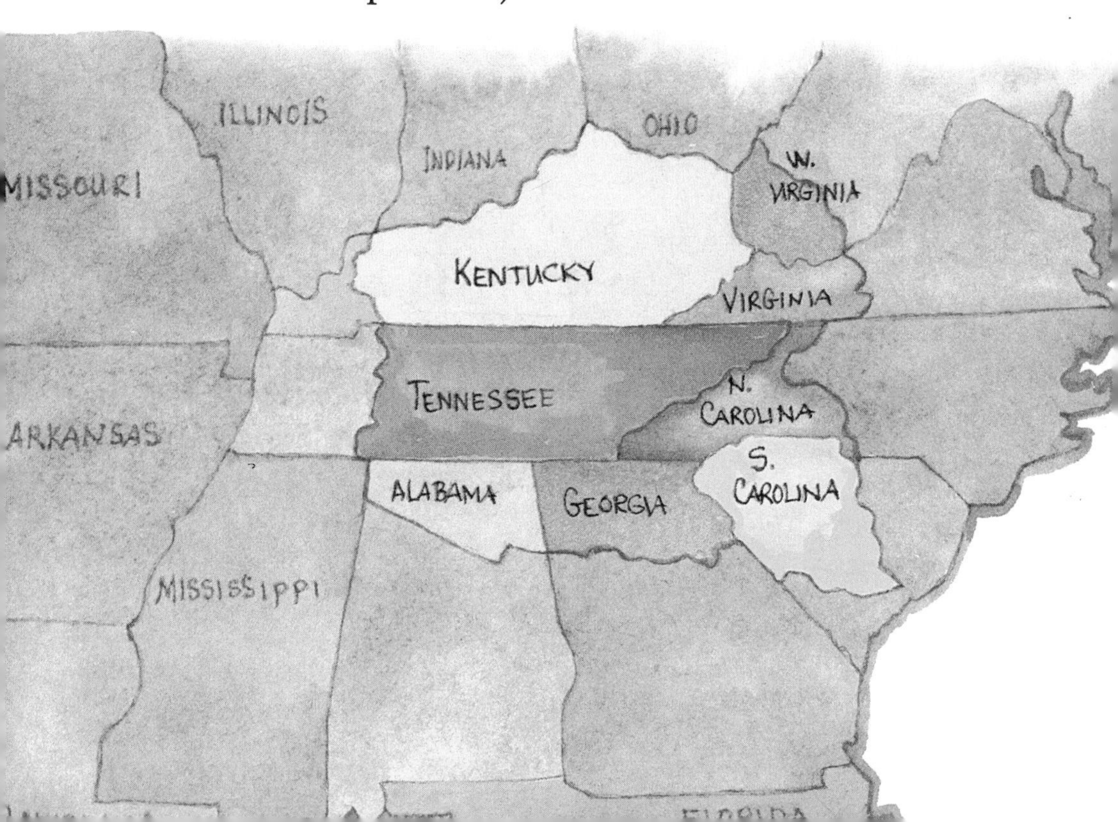

When white settlers first came from Europe, the Cherokees tried to live in peace with them. For over a hundred years, Cherokees traded with English colonists. Some Cherokee leaders even went to England to visit the king.

Then the American Revolution was fought between the British and the American colonists. When the war was over, American settlers wanted the land owned by Cherokees. There was more fighting, this time against the Cherokees. A thousand Cherokee towns were destroyed. The Cherokees gave up some of their land. In return, the United States promised to always protect the Cherokees.

The Cherokee Nation wanted to live in peace with the United States. It moved its capital south to New Echota, Georgia. The Cherokees began to adopt more white ways. Many Cherokees became wealthy. They had plantation houses, sawmills, and large herds of cattle. Some Cherokee men went to schools in New England. The Cherokees even invented a written language all their own.

In 1821, a man named Sequoyah shared this great invention with his people. For many years, he had sought a way to write down the Cherokee language. Finally, he succeeded in creating a Cherokee alphabet. Each symbol stood for a sound in Cherokee.

His little daughter, Ahyokah, helped him. She was the first person Sequoyah taught. At first, other Cherokees did not believe that Sequoyah could really write their language. Only the white people could make "talking leaves," as the Cherokees called writing on paper. But whatever message Sequoyah wrote down, Ahyokah could read. No other person in human history had ever created a new alphabet all alone. If you spoke Cherokee, you could now easily learn to write it. Soon almost every Cherokee person could read and write.

In 1827, the Cherokee Nation founded its own newspaper, printed in both English and Cherokee. It was called *Tsa-la-gi Tsu-le-hi-sah-nuh-hi.*

ᏣᎳᎩ ᏧᎴᎯ ᏌᏅᎯ

Those words mean "Cherokee will rise again." In English, it is the *Cherokee Phoenix,* named for the mythical bird that rises from its own ashes. It was clear that the Cherokees had made the most of peace. But that peace would not last.

Going West

The more the Cherokees succeeded, the more enemies they made. Many people did not want them around. They wanted Cherokee land for themselves. President Thomas Jefferson believed in a policy called Indian Removal. This meant moving all Indians to Indian Territory, the lands west of the Mississippi River. Jefferson thought this policy would protect the Indians from dishonest white people who might trick them or kill them for their land. It would also open up the former Indian land to white settlers.

President Jefferson said it would take a thousand years for Americans to settle the West. Indian Territory would be Indian land forever. But Jefferson was wrong. It would take less than a hundred years for the West to be settled. And there was no "open land" in Indian Territory. It was already occupied by other Native Americans.

Most Cherokees opposed giving up their land. Some Cherokees, though, including Sequoyah, decided to go west. They established new towns in Arkansas. It was not easy. The Indians who were already there made war on them. White settlers complained that the Indians had the best land. But the Arkansas Cherokees succeeded. They established schools and a formal government.

Their stay in Arkansas lasted ten years. Then the Arkansas Cherokees were forced into a new treaty. They moved farther west to Oklahoma.

Most Cherokees, though, chose to stay in the East. It was their home. They would not give it up without a fight. By 1828, Cherokee territory was only a tenth of its former size. Other tribes had all been forced west. But 17,000 Cherokees remained.

The Cherokee Republic created a new government modeled after the United States. John Ross was chosen to be the Principal Chief. He vowed to protect his people's right to their land.

It was not easy. In 1828, Andrew Jackson was elected president of the United States. In his first address to Congress, President Jackson said that all Indians must now be removed. During the War of 1812, when General Jackson was fighting the British, many Cherokee volunteers had fought by his side. Two of those loyal Cherokees were Sequoyah and John Ross. But Jackson didn't care that Cherokees had helped him in the past. He sponsored the Indian Removal Bill.

Things quickly got worse for the Cherokees. Gold was discovered on Cherokee lands in Georgia. Georgia created anti-Indian laws. Similar laws were passed in Alabama. It was now illegal for one Cherokee to try to persuade another to stay on his own land. It was even illegal for Cherokees to dig for gold on their *own* land.

The state of Georgia divided the Cherokee Republic into land lots. It set up a lottery to give those lots away to white men. Cherokee families came home to discover that everything they owned had been taken. These state anti-Indian laws broke agreements the United States government had made with the Cherokees.

The Cherokees fought for their rights in court. John Ross traveled back and forth to Washington, D.C. In 1832, the Supreme Court ruled in favor of the Cherokee Nation. But President Jackson sided with the Southern states. He allowed them to ignore the Supreme Court.

One night, Chief John Ross returned from Washington to find that his own plantation had been taken over by lottery winners. The new white owners said that he could spend the night. However, he had to pay a fee to stay in his own house! The next day, he looked for his family. He found his wife, Quatie, and their two little children on the road to Tennessee, soaked by the rain.

But despite the pressure from the Southern states, nearly all Cherokees were still determined to keep their land. However, the Cherokees were not completely united. A small group of wealthy Cherokees disagreed.

They thought life was too hard for the Cherokee people in the East. Going west might be the only way for the Cherokees to survive. And so they made a decision. Some Cherokees thought it was a brave decision. Many others thought it was a bad decision made by bad men.

This small group of Cherokees met with representatives of the United States government. They had no right to speak for their people as a whole. However, they signed a treaty agreeing to the western removal of the entire Cherokee Nation.

John Ross and the official representatives of the Cherokees said this treaty was illegal. Former president John Quincy Adams said that the treaty "brings disgrace upon the country." However, the United States Senate approved it by a single vote. A smile of victory on his face, President Andrew Jackson signed the Treaty of New Echota into law. The removal of the Cherokees would go into effect in 1838. The Cherokees were about to walk the Trail of Tears.

The Place Where the People Cried

Only twenty Cherokee men signed the Treaty of New Echota. John Ross went to Washington with a petition signed by 16,000 Cherokee people who opposed the treaty. The western Cherokees sent another petition to Congress signed by Sequoyah and the other western Cherokee leaders. Many white Americans supported the Cherokees as well. They wrote articles in newspapers and sent letters and petitions. The letters and petitions and pleas were all ignored.

Some Cherokees went west before the deadline of May 1838. The men who signed the treaty led small groups of Cherokee settlers to what is now the state of Oklahoma. They picked out the best homesites for themselves.

Martin Van Buren was now president of the United States. He feared that the remaining Cherokees would try to fight. He sent General John Ellis Wool to take away their weapons. But the general found himself protecting the Cherokee people instead. Dishonest white men were flocking to Cherokee land to cheat the Cherokees and steal from them. These white men, Wool said, "are like vultures...ready to pounce."

General Wool resigned in protest. Georgia threatened to go to war against the Cherokee people if the Cherokees were not removed. President Van Buren did not wish to anger the South. He sent General Winfield Scott to take Wool's place. Scott's army rounded up the Cherokees.

Almost all the Cherokee people were taken captive. They were locked up in stockade forts. They had to leave behind everything except for the clothes they wore and what little they could carry. Groups of white men, following the soldiers, quickly took over the Cherokee homes.

Families were separated as people were herded into the camps. Children cried out for their parents. Frantic mothers looked for their little ones. Food and water were scarce. People began to get sick. Many died while being held captive. They were prisoners whose only crime was that they were Cherokees and white people wanted their land.

Several routes were used to take the Cherokees west. One was by water. People were loaded onto large flatboats guarded by troops. On the crowded boats, more people became sick. Some fell into the water and drowned.

The other routes were mostly by land. They were longer, but safer.

When Chief John Ross returned again from Washington, he was upset by what he saw. In the crowded camps there was no bedding and no cooking utensils. There was no protection from the burning summer sun or the rains. Some people were nearly naked. Cherokees were dying in great numbers.

Chief John Ross made a proposal to General Scott. Instead of treating the Cherokees like criminals and forcing them to move, he asked Scott to let the Cherokee people arrange their own travel west.

No other group of Indians had been allowed to do this. They had all been escorted to Indian Territory by United States troops. But Scott was upset by what had happened to the Cherokees. To everyone's surprise, he agreed.

Ex-president Andrew Jackson was enraged. He wrote an angry letter to the United States Attorney General in protest. However, John Ross's plan was allowed to go on.

Each Cherokee was given an allowance of $65.88. This would cover the cost of wagons, horses and oxen, bedding, food, soap, and clothing. They would also have to pay to use the turnpikes—private roads whose owners demanded money for their use.

The Cherokees divided into parties. They would follow the long land route. They hoped to travel fifteen miles each day. That way, they would make the 1,200-mile trip in eighty days. Because of the heat, the start was delayed. The first group left on October 1, 1838. The last group departed on November 7. They had months of travel ahead of them.

The Cherokee people had been through a lot. But their troubles were not yet over. They feared that the roll of thunder and the black cloud at the start of their journey were bad omens. Those fears turned out to be true. White men followed the wagon trains, trying to steal from them. Cherokees were charged more than anyone else for using roads and ferries. Many were still sick from living in the camps. Wagons broke down. Horses and oxen died. Winter weather came early.

Quatie, the wife of John Ross, was very ill. But when she saw a sick child shivering by the road, she gave the child her blanket. On February 1, 1839, John Ross paused to bury Quatie near Little Rock, Arkansas. There were many such deaths.

The legend of the Cherokee Rose grew from the Trail of Tears. It is said that each drop of blood that fell from the Cherokees turned into a stone rose. Those red stone crystals can still be found along the Arkansas River. In 1968, the Cherokee Rose was made the state stone of Oklahoma.

No one knows how many died during the removal. Some say it was 4,000 or more. It is no wonder that the Cherokees still call this terrible experience *nuna dat shun'yi,* "the Place Where They Cried"—The Trail of Tears. The last Cherokee party arrived in Indian Territory on March 25, 1839. Their hard journey had taken 139 days. The Trail of Tears was over. But the long road toward healing the people's wounds had just begun.

At the End of the Trail

When the Cherokees arrived in Indian Territory, they found little to welcome them. Nearby tribes were suffering from smallpox. Land given to the Cherokees was already occupied by others. Supplies promised by the United States government did not arrive. The eastern Cherokee people, led by John Ross, wanted to keep their government. The western Cherokees, who had moved to Indian Territory long before the Trail of Tears, did not want to be governed by the newcomers.

Many blamed their suffering on those who had signed the Treaty of New Echota. On June 22, 1839, some of the men who signed the treaty were killed.

John Ross, Sequoyah, and other Cherokee leaders worked to restore calm to their divided nation. Councils were held. A single Cherokee Nation was created, uniting old settlers and new immigrants.

For almost two decades, the Cherokee Nation prospered. A capital was established with stores, a hotel, and a brick Supreme Court building. A newspaper, the *Cherokee Advocate,* was founded. By 1856, there were twenty-one Cherokee elementary and secondary schools for both men and women. Latin, algebra, botany, grammar, and geography were among the subjects all Cherokee students were required to take. The Cherokee Nation in Indian Territory had become a model of success.

The Cherokees Today

The Cherokee Nation still survives today. In fact, two Cherokee Nations exist. One is in Oklahoma. The other is in the old Cherokee homelands of North Carolina.

Despite the efforts of the United States Army, not all Cherokees went west. Some hid from the army in wooded areas. This was especially true in the rugged Great Smoky Mountains of western North Carolina.

Others escaped from the camps. Troops

were sent to recapture them, but some Cherokees resisted. Two white soldiers were killed. One of the Cherokees, an old man named Tsali, was sentenced to death after he and two of his sons killed a soldier trying to capture them. He was killed by a firing squad of his own people. They knew that they would be shot if they didn't obey. Tsali showed such bravery that he became a folk hero.

In all, over 1,000 Cherokees stayed in the mountains of North Carolina. Eventually, the United States government gave them permission to remain on a small reservation. Today there are over 10,000 members in the Eastern Band of Cherokee in North Carolina. Each year, a pageant called "Unto These Hills," based on the Trail of Tears and the story of Tsali, is performed in Cherokee, North Carolina.

In Oklahoma, the Cherokees survived as well. They did so in spite of the hardships of the Trail of Tears. The western Cherokees of Oklahoma now number over 80,000. They have a thriving tribal government, schools for Cherokee children, and businesses that employ Cherokee people.

Lessons can be learned from the bitter journey called the Trail of Tears. One is that when promises are broken, many people may suffer. There is another lesson, however, to be learned from the place where the people cried. It is a lesson of hope. The Cherokees showed us the importance of courage and determination. Their survival is the survival of all that is best in the human spirit.